Dear Parents:

Here's a book that we're excited to be sharing with you.

This is different from most books you will receive as members of the Weekly Reader Children's Book Club. While this is a fun picture book to read, it also is a book with a mission. Already, *Publisher's Weekly* has praised this book as a "forceful environmental guide for the youngest readers." What makes this book so appealing is the cast of characters that Laurie and Marc Brown have created. The delightful creatures from their two earlier books, *Dinosaurs Alive and Well!* and *Dinosaurs Divorce* share their most critical message yet: Save the environment!

This is the kind of book that will probably evoke a lot of discussion at home. For instance, what can we do to save Mother Earth? Even the youngest family members will want to do their part. And, who can resist the Slobosaurus?

Sincerely,

Stephen Fraser

Stephen Fraser
Senior Editor
Weekly Reader Books

Weekly Reader Children's Book Club Presents

DINOSAURS
TO THE RESCUE!

A Guide to Protecting Our Planet

Laurie Krasny Brown and Marc Brown

Little, Brown and Company
Boston   Toronto   London

JOY STREET BOOKS

For Mike and Ann Shilhan,
who take such beautiful care of their place on the planet

Our special thanks to Michelle Brauner, environmental consultant;
Carol Cirillo, teacher, Belmont Day School; Dr. Verne Howe,
chairwoman, North American Association of Environmental Educators;
Ingrid Kavanagh, founder, Children's Alliance for the Protection of the
Environment; Doug Smith, exhibitions planner, Boston Museum of
Science; and his son, Gregory Smith, student in elementary school.

This book is a presentation of Newfield Publications, Inc.
Newfield Publications offers book clubs for
children from preschool through high school.
For more information write to:
Newfield Publications, Inc.
4343 Equity Drive, Columbus, Ohio 43228.

Reprinted by arrangement with Little, Brown and Company (Inc.).
Newfield Publications is a trademark
of Newfield Publications, Inc.
Weekly Reader is a federally registered trademark
of Weekly Reader Corporation.

First Edition

Library of Congress Cataloging-in-Publication Data

Brown, Laurene Krasny.
Dinosaurs to the rescue!: a guide to protecting our planet/
Laurie Krasny Brown and Marc Brown. — 1st ed.
    p.   cm.
  Summary: Text and illustrations of dinosaur characters introduce
the earth's major environmental problems and suggest ways children
can help.
  ISBN 0-316-11087-6
  1. Environmental protection — Citizen participation — Juvenile
literature. [1. Environmental protection.] I. Brown, Marc Tolon.
II. Title.
TD171.7B76   1992
333.7'2 — dc20   91-27177
                    10 9 8 7 6 5 4 3 2 1
                              WOR
Joy Street Books are published by Little, Brown and Company (Inc.)
Published simultaneously in Canada by Little, Brown & Company (Canada) Limited
Printed in the United States of America

Earth is the only home we have!
Every day our planet offers us fresh air, clean water, and fertile land. But these gifts, called natural resources, won't always be here if we waste or spoil them.
There are many ways we can all help protect our planet!

Use Less

Using only as much as you need of the earth's resources is one way to help. By wasting less, you leave more for tomorrow and for others, too.

Water   We couldn't live without it!
We drink it, cook with it, and use it to wash ourselves and other things. All plants and animals need water to grow and stay healthy.
You can help save water — just turn it off!

Turn off the water while brushing your teeth. A gallon is wasted every minute the faucet is on.

Taking a bath can use up 50 gallons of water. That's 800 glasses!

A water-saving showerhead helps use less water, too!

Only run a full dishwasher. Or when you hand-wash dishes, use a basin of soapy water instead of running the tap.

Electricity

Every time you or your parents turn something on — lights, heat, the stove, or the car — it uses up energy. You can save energy by turning these things on only when you need them — and turning them off when you are done.

Opening the refrigerator lets in warm air and wastes electricity. Try to get what you need quickly and then close the door.

Cool off in hot weather by opening windows and curtains at night. Use a fan instead of an air conditioner, which puts harmful gases into the air.

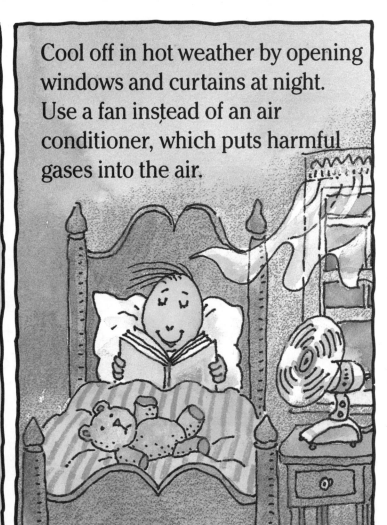

Use your own energy whenever you can.

Cars   The smoke that comes from driving a car pollutes the air by making it dirty and hard to breathe. Share car rides whenever you can, and use other ways to get around.

Paper   Trees are natural resources, too. They give us everything from cleaner air, shade, wood, fruit, and nuts to the material for making paper. Trees offer homes for birds and other animals, too.

You can help save trees by using less paper. Use paper up completely before throwing it out or recycling it.

I can squeeze on a few more words....

Instead of paper plates and cups, choose dishes and glasses you can wash and use again and again.

Wipe up spills with a reusable sponge or cloth instead of paper towels, which have to be thrown away.

Bring along your own bag or backpack to carry home what you buy at the store.

No, thanks! I brought my own bag.

Plastic   Plastic is made from one of the earth's buried resources — oil. If we use up all the oil that's under the ground, there won't be any more!

You can save oil by using less plastic. So many things come wrapped in plastic that just gets thrown away. Take home as little plastic as you can.

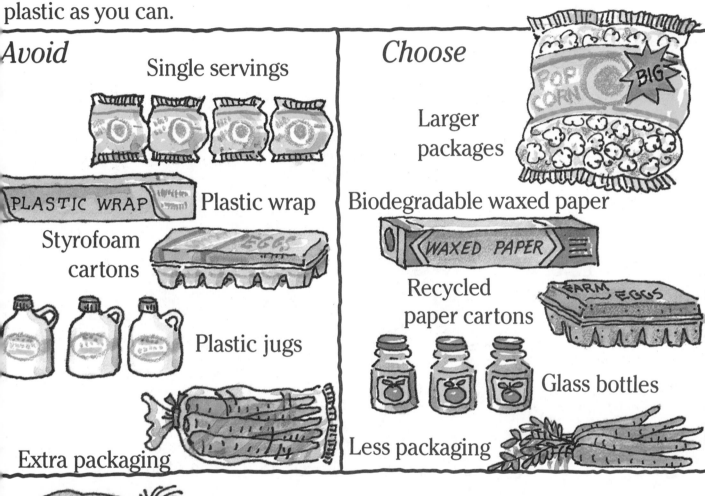

Avoid

Single servings

Plastic wrap

Styrofoam cartons

Plastic jugs

Extra packaging

Choose

Larger packages

Biodegradable waxed paper

Recycled paper cartons

Glass bottles

Less packaging

If you're looking for a snack, try one that doesn't come in plastic but in its own natural package — it's biodegradable.

Use Again

Another way to protect natural resources is to reuse the things you have. Reusing things saves the energy and materials it takes to make new ones. It also pollutes less and leaves less to throw away.

Taking care of toys and supplies helps them last longer.

New Uses

Try finding new uses for things instead of throwing them aw

Turn an old shoe box into a place to keep something special.

Save colorful paper scraps to make cards for your family and friends. Make wrapping paper by decorating newspaper.

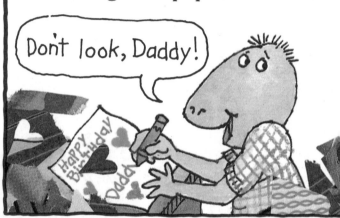

Use plastic containers to hold things for picnics or to play with in the tub or at the beach.

You can even make your whole Halloween costume from things you recycle!

Recycling Recycling garbage begins at home. Materials such as glass, metals, and paper can be remade into new recycled products. All you need are boxes or bags for collecting the things your city or town recycles.

New Homes

Finding new homes for things you outgrow allows others to use and enjoy them, too.
You may want to give things away to a hospital or shelter.

Every time you begin to throw something away, stop and think,
Is there some way I can reuse this?

Give Something Back

The earth keeps us alive. But we can't just take from it all the time. We also need to give something back. You can help by doing all you can to make the outdoors clean and safe.

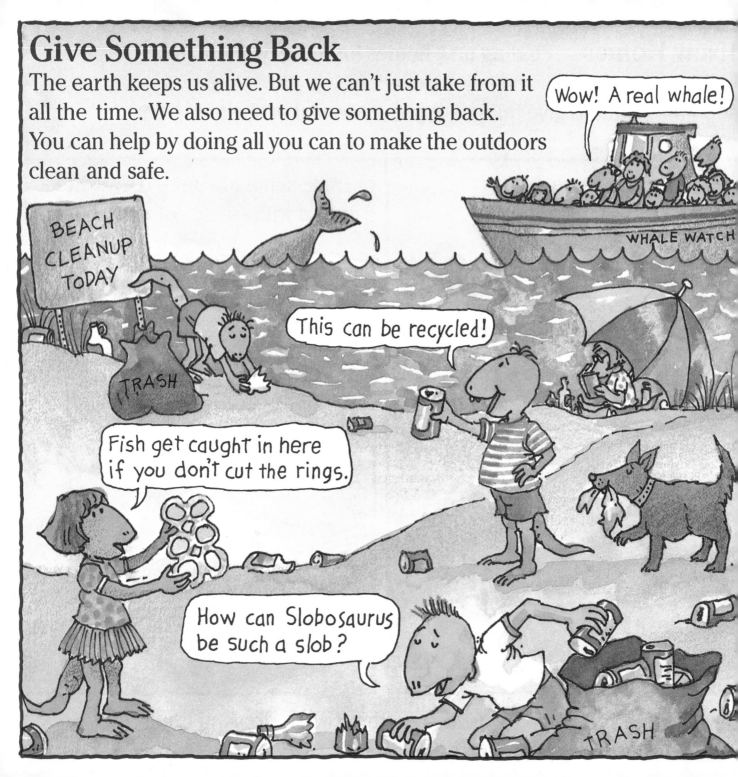

Throw garbage in litter baskets. Plastic trash can harm animals.

Marking up buildings and walls is a way of trashing them. Help keep them clean.

Cleaning up after your dog makes the streets a nicer and healthier place to be.

Pick up litter wherever you find it!

You can help save the lives of animals and plants. Each one has a reason for being and a unique place in nature.
If you catch an animal or insect, don't keep it. Try to put it back where you found it.

Appreciating plants and animals without taking them home protects nature and leaves them for you and others to enjoy again.

Grow something at home. Every plant helps make the air cleaner and our earth greener.

Every little thing you do to take care of our Earth makes a difference!